sitting by the rapids

ALBERT DUMONT

KEGEDONCE PRESS
2018

October 2018

Published by Kegedonce Press
11 Park Road, Neyaashiinigmiing, ON N0H 2T0
www.kegedonce.com

Administration Office/Book Orders
P.O. Box 517, Owen Sound, ON N4K 5R1

Printed in Canada by Sotek Graphics
Cover Art: Catherine Dallaire
Back Cover Author Photo: Jason Pickering
Art Direction: Kateri Akiwenzie-Damm
Design: Chantal Lalonde Design

Library and Archives Canada Cataloguing in Publication

Dumont, Albert, 1950-, author
    Sitting by the rapids / Albert Dumont.

Poems.
ISBN 978-1-928120-17-9 (softcover)

        I. Title.

PS8557.U532S58 2018   C811'.6   C2018-905747-5

For Customer Service/Orders
Tel 1-800-591-6250 Fax 1-800-591-6251
100 Armstrong Ave. Georgetown, ON L7G 5S4
Email orders@litdistco.ca

We acknowledge the support of the Canada Council for the Arts, which last
year invested $153 million to bring the arts to Canadians throughout the
country.

Canada Council   Conseil des arts
for the Arts   du Canada

We would like to acknowledge funding support from the Ontario Arts
Council, an agency of the Government of Ontario.

ONTARIO ARTS COUNCIL
CONSEIL DES ARTS DE L'ONTARIO
an Ontario government agency
un organisme du gouvernement de l'Ontario

table of contents

HEALING

SPIRITUALITY

BLOODLINE

SEASONS

TREES

HEALING

because of you

The Words of the Victim

You pushed me into raging waters
And I wonder
If I will ever be the same

Because of you
I have forgotten the reasons
For the blossoms
And the purpose of the rain

Because of you
Instead of smiling into the dawn
I hide
And shed tear after tear

Because of you
I feel as the rust
That descends onto the beauty
Of the autumn's maple leaves

Because of you
Peace eludes me
And I know only heartache
Everywhere I turn

It is good that you tell me
That you are sorry
But tell me also
What you will do that will
Restore who and what I was
Before your cruelty
Pushed me into raging waters

because of me

I pushed you into raging waters
And now I wonder
If you will ever be the same

Because of me
You have forgotten the reasons
For the blossoms
And the purpose of the rain

Because of me
Instead of smiling into the dawn
You hide
And shed tear after tear

Because of me
You feel as the rust
That descends onto the beauty
Of the autumn's maple leaves

Because of me
Peace eludes you
And you know only heartache
Everywhere you turn

I regret that I have caused you
Such great suffering
And I am sorry

What would you have me do
That would help you
Restore who and what you were
Before my cruelty
Pushed you into raging waters

pain

You tell me that
You look to drugs to relieve you
Of the pain which constantly consumes you
The pain brought into your life
Because of fractured bones and unresolved grief
The pain brought into your life
Because of the negligence you say
I am guilty of

Your pain is great
And I acknowledge that you have a right
To free yourself of it
In any manner you see fit
But I ask
That you think now and then
Of the great emotional pain
Your addiction to drugs
Brings into the heart and soul
Of those who love you
I would rather have my heart
Crushed in a vice than to
See you strung out on heroin
Please, make a vow of sobriety
And free me at last
Of this torturous existence

I want you to live
I want to see you dance again
Never forget that love is healing
Never forget how much I love you

a thousand lives

I have not lived a thousand lives
But I sometimes feel
Like I have died a thousand deaths

Mangled, killed and butchered
My spirit hung up to dry

My heart broken into tiny pieces
All because I fell in love

In prayer and ceremony, my heart
Opens like a flower's petals
To receive the wisdom
Of the rising sun

And the healing medicine
Of all my relations
Arrives in my circle
Reassuring me

I will survive

where is the bird

Where is the lake
I can wade into
And emerge
My heart filled with righteousness

Where is the trail
In the thick woods
Leading to the circle
Where my spirit
Can replenish itself with courage and truth

Where is the bird
Which would lift me upon its back
So I can fly with it
Searching for the place
Where I can discover again
Purpose and a reinvigorated sense of humanity

My friend, the lake you search for
Is any of your territory

The trail leading to the circle
Is the only trail necessary

The bird you seek
Is the eagle

It calls to you

home

Home is
Sitting by the rapids
Watching bubbling waters
Washing over rocks
Through tear-filled eyes

Home is
Sitting by the rapids
Listening to the song of the river
Your heart, filled with laughter and joy

four eagles

Four eagles will descend
From a sky made bright
By spirit beings

And I will soar
With them
My body free of suffering
My soul free of sin

I will visit again, those joyful places
Of the people
I have grown to love
So they will know without a doubt
The true friend
That I
Have always been

cancer

Cancer eats at your organs
Weakens you physically
Drains you of purpose

Alcohol is like a cancer

It ate at my spirit
It shredded my desire
To become a better human being

Somehow, I chased alcohol from my life
I stand now
Proudly, under the sun
At peace before the pines

In harmony with the birds
I make my vow, alcohol
Will never again pass my lips

panic attack

It begins lightning quick
A feeling, that I
No longer have control of my senses
Like a bird
His breast pierced by the hunter's arrow
Descending from a turbulent sky
His mind racing, confused, frightened
His heart, wildly beating
As if inside of a hollow barrel

anxiety

Suddenly, I am overcome with a sensation
As if floating on an angry sea
Searching, searching
For an island on which to rest
To find a caring hand and solitude

I am sure I am dying
I want to scream goodbye, goodbye
To my loving family and dearest friends

An island, o God
Where is an island?

I wait to die
But the sea calms
And I become aware
That I will, after all, survive

they are here

They are here among us
The people who worship the Almighty Dollar
They bring sickness and death
To our precious waters
They poison the land
And the grass decays before our eyes
They cut all the trees
And leave the moose without a range
They destroy the chance
Of long lives for our grandchildren

The people who worship the Almighty Dollar
They are here

the voices of the city

When the voices
Of the city come ringing out
Fire trucks, police sirens
The yells of road rage

I gather my drum and medicines
To travel with the smoke
Of smouldering sage
And with the song of my drum
To my place
Of healing and peaceful meditation

In my mind
I see you preparing cake
I see you honouring the life
Flourishing on Bitobi Lake
I see the smile on your face
When I bathe your feet with cedar water

These are things I think about
When the voices
Of the city come ringing out

our strong people

Like a cloud
Pushed swiftly by the wind
From one horizon to the other
Unnoticed by human eyes

The good deeds
And honourable actions
Of our strong people soar

For them, an honour song
Is spiritually heard

recovery

In the winds of a dying desert
I stand, looking into a sky
Empty of hawks and eagles

O Great Spirit
Only Your eyes can see
The wounds which crushed my spirit
Long ago when I was lost
I ask today that You continue
To bless my place
In the sacred circle
Until I am at long last, again
A proud son of my people

i see it

I point my face
Towards the sun
My eyes tightly shut
Still I see
All the colours of a magnificent sunrise
Like the fire within the fire
The heart and spirit of the day
I see it

what is a man

What is a man
Who no longer smiles
When hearing the songs of birds
Emerging from the forest

Who no longer honours the trees
As wiser beings than himself

Who no longer longs to walk
Barefoot in the rain

Such a man has been swallowed up
By his own ego and selfishness
He has doomed himself to live
Only as a machine, forever running away
From his duties and responsibilities

SPIRITUALITY

in honour of water

Great Spirit
Swiftly would all things die
If the waters of our country
Were to disappear

The medicine waters of spring
The water in the thawing earth

The rains which remove the snow and ice
Which blanket the sleeping rivers
So brightness can enter again
Into the world where the fish live

The waters of
The chanting creeks and streams
Which carry away the last faint whispers
Of winter's soft spiritual messages

My heart fills with despair
To think of waters forever gone
Show us again, Creator, the ways
To defend and honour water

the fasting circle

It is my guiding light
O, I sing and dance
Within its boundaries
O, I weep with joy
When my ancestors visit

When dark clouds
Cover the moon and stars
Still, I see the universe
Sitting by the fire
Of my fasting circle

a prayer

O Great Spirit
Into a gentle breeze I softly sing
And I rise to dance in thanksgiving
That You have created human beings
I promise to continue each dawn
To heap praise on the goodness
You have placed before the Peoples
To teach us, to feed us
To nurture and sustain us

The great trees growing
Out of a narrow blanket of earth
Covering the rocky hillside

The small bird flying against ferocious winds

The sparkles of playful fish
Under dark, ice-covered waters

The sun, the wind and waters
Which grant us joyful lives

For them
I rise to dance in thanksgiving

For I am aware
That if not for them, the drumming
Of human hearts would forever fall silent

the sacred fire

It is spiritually alive
It pulses and vibrates
The colours it sends forth
Dance with the shrubs
And illuminate
The trees around it

It is a holy circle
Into which
Darkness is not welcome

BLOODLINE

when i look at you

When I look at you
I see a strong woman
Wise beyond her years

I see you dance with pride
And graceful movement
That quells my spirit's fears

I see you bathe in the fragrance
Of the sweetgrass, the cedar and the sage
Earnest purifications of your being
To prevent an inner rage

I see you shun temptation
When the drum reaches to your ears
When I look at you
I see a strong woman
Wise beyond her years

slivers

Slivers from my family tree
Asking me

Grandpa, can a river die
Grandpa, who would make a river cry
I think about the sturgeon and the eels
And I wonder how they feel
Grandpa, it's like a terrible dream
To know poisons enter into a stream

Grandpa, have you ever killed a river
The question of my family sliver

today

Dedicated to our Tiny Children

Today
We are blossoms on a tree
We are the tiniest fish, swimming free
We are a fawn on wobbly legs
We are a featherless bird
Just emerged from the egg

We are the springtime of the year
We are the sunrise of the day

But tomorrow
Tomorrow we will spiritually soar
With the things of Creator's love
We will not forget their noble song
We will not forget their noble song

my parents

In Honour of Loving Parents

I close my eyes
And drift away on sacred memories

I see the fish of spring
Releasing her eggs into swift moving waters

I see the black bear of summer
Side by side with her cub

From the autumn sky
I hear the voices of southbound geese

In the silence of winter
A sacred fire burns, in the smoke
A prayer climbs the shining sky

The blood of my heart
Is sweet with the love and respect
I have for you, my parents

our young people

Our young people
Who surround themselves with Indigenous wisdom
Are like the dawning
Of a long anticipated spring

They will not be stopped

memories

After the drumming of my heart
Has fallen silent
And the memories I held so dear
Have been placed
Into the care of my future generations
I will awaken into a world anew
Where my ancestors will greet me
With honour songs and vibrating rattles
A great feast will take place
And forevermore
I will be surrounded
By love, peace and kindness

i remember

I remember
A troubled young man
His heart hollow of spiritual substance
His spirit
In a constant state of despair
Always feeling helpless and out of balance
His heart, mind and spirit
Unable to see
The true glory of what it means
To be a human being

Today, that young man
Is an old man
He stands in the circle
The partridge by his side
The blackberry moon, guiding his life

the heart

The heart
Though physically small
Can hold
An army of fearless defenders
Ready to protect the fire
Of our healing circle

It is a mountain
The bloodline climbs
To sing as one
On its spiritual summit

i walk among them

I walk among them
The people of a foreign nation
Without eagle feathers
In my hair
Without moose hide moccasins
On my feet

I do not chant
The songs of my grandfathers
Nor ride a spotted pony

And because of this
They tell me
"You do not look Native Indian"

the victim

In Memory of Teddy Bellingham (1976-1992)

He would often wonder who he was
He did not know his clan
He never smoked the sacred pipe
Or danced upon the land
He did not know about the drum
Or know where eagles fly
He died without a chance for knowledge
It makes the elders cry

This boy, so violently killed
Failed by settler guardians
Unable to give him love
Unable to contribute to his identity

He journeyed into the spirit world
Without a spirit name
The ancestors who met him there
Comfort and love him all the same

my brother

I see in the distance a line of smoke
Ascending above the tallest trees
From the mountain where my brother hunts
But he is far away

I draw in a breath
To take in the aroma of the game
My brother cooks
But it is useless
He is far away

I call his name with all the force granted me
As a human being
But my brother will not hear my cry
He is far away

Only my heart can travel to where he is
To hear his voice
To sit in counsel with him

Only my spirit will again, one day
Hunt and feast with him
My brother

look at my life
and see my strengths

Inspired by Residential School Survivor Helen Thompson

Under the frozen moon of February
A harsh life for me began
But I found peace and solitude
Where the deer and rabbits ran

Taken as a girl from loved ones
To Canada's cruel Residential School
Where I was made to forget
The wisdom of the forest
And the spirit of the land

Always sharing what little I had
With precious family and my dearest friends
I promise to love you unconditionally
Until time comes to its trembling end

In the land of souls
I urge you
To look at my life
And see my strengths

a sacred treaty

A sacred treaty
Between the People and the fur-bearing animals
Was made when the hills were young

The animals promised
To look after the People
To feed and clothe them
And to do their part
In keeping a perfect balance
In the sacred cycle of life

The People, in return
Promised to always honour and respect
Their fur-bearing relatives
To never kill them without purpose
And to never waste of their bodies

All was well
The People
Were strong and healthy and lived joyful lives

But then one day, a stranger arrived
He said "Bring me the fur
Of your brother the beaver and I
Will give you guns and steel kettles"
The People did as the stranger requested
Thus began the fur trade
Thus began the destruction of our ways
The sacred treaty made long ago
With the animals, was broken
And with that
A relentless storm arrived

We call to Creator
For a chance, to once again
Be at peace
With our fur-bearing relatives
We ask for their forgiveness
We ask that
The sacred treaty with them
Be brought back to life
Our very identity depends on it

our girls

A pearl, a girl
A wind that whirls

Talk of love, of a dove
Of God up above

Teddy bears, country fairs
Doing things on a dare

Giggles and wiggles
And twinkles in the eye

A sigh, a good cry

A song about "What's wrong!"
A circle in which to belong

A friend to the end
A shield that never bends

A plan for a clan
A wife and her man

Pow wow dancing, models prancing
Handsome boys glancing

Enter the evil
Our greatest fear
Our girls disappear

the eyes of
little children

A little bird has told me
That the winged creatures of the land
Are evermore
Losing their faith in human beings

A fish has told me
That the waters are evermore being poisoned

A tree has told me
That the forest is slowly dying

The eyes of little children, tell us
"Do something about it"

i love you

I love you
Not as I would
If you were my sister
I love you
Not as I would
If you were my lover

I love you
Because of the love you have
For the waters of my homeland
I love you
Because you are strong
And bow before no man

SEASONS

the raspberry moon

The raspberry moon is old
Yet keeps its strength and vigour
Overly ripened berries fall
The stem, no longer
Possessing the ability to hold them

In the berry patch
An old man fills his basket
The sun presses on his naked back
A tear runs from his eye

His mind wanders to long ago times
When he was young and selfish
When he was lost and confused
When his life was without purpose

He places tobacco on the land
And continues to fill his basket

The raspberry moon is old
Yet it keeps its strength and vigour

early spring

Swirling, bitter winds
Descended from the hills
Bringing shivering temperatures
Into my lonely bed
All I could do
Was hug my old worn-out pillow
And make-believe
At least for a moment
That it was you

I thought, only April now
Only a month since you left
I thought, how will I survive?
I prayed, Creator tell me how

Then I recalled a white pine tree
Pointing to the east, who said
"With tomorrow comes a new dawn
A day to start life afresh"

where berries grow

In the wild berry patch
We find
The generosity and sweetness
Of our Creator

Where berries grow
We find the reasons for
Why a promise should never be broken

Where berries grow
We find the teachings, instructing us
To defend and protect
What was given to us by Creator

Where berries grow
We realize that death
Does not stop
The love
Of deceased relatives
From surrounding us
When our hearts are heavy
With despair and anguish

man of the blackberry moon

In the song of the rapids
And in the stirring of leaves
He heard the voices of medicine beings
"Your spirit is strong" they told him
"You will survive"

The teachings of the blackberry moon
Entered his soul
And his spirit filled with ancestral wisdom

His heart became a guardian
Of sacred knowledge
And he realized
His duty as a protector
And the need
For balance in all things

O Grandfather
Your heart beats in harmony with mine
Your counsels repel the winds of despair
Your blood warms
The blood of my children
You stand in the centre
Of our circle
And so it will be forevermore, forevermore

autumn woman

Songbirds and red maple leaves
No longer seen
Leaving the spirit of the mournful land
To accept her loss with dignity

You, born in late autumn, are sacred
In your own special way

Whose tears are more real than yours?
Whose truthful words are more sought after
Than the words of women
Born in the late autumn of the year

spring

The energies of Mother Earth
Rise, taking their places in the circle

Spring spirit vibrates in the hills and valleys
Mixing with the songs of birds
And the melody
Of fast flowing waters

Hope and renewal
Descend like falling rain
To fill the hearts
Of emotionally troubled human beings

It is Spring
A time to awaken our bodies
And to refresh in the circle
The spirit of our sacred bundles

TREES

when the cedar
is gone

When the cedar is gone
Who then, will speak of our spirituality
When the oak is gone
Who then, will speak of our strength
When the maple is gone
Who then, will speak of our generosity
When the birch is gone
Who then, will speak of our creativity
When the pine is gone
Who then, will speak of our legends

like trees

In Honour of Loving Parents

Like trees
Sheltering the life of the forest
You have always stood strong
Protecting me from destructive winds
A thousand winters of wisdom
You place on my life's pathway
Nourishing me, your hand I take
Your smiles I bring into my dreams

The joys and sorrows of your past
You send forth like birds
Sunlight dancing on their wings, they come
Shielding my heart and mind
From all which would crush my spirit

The spirit of the land
Locks like an unbreakable cord
With the commitment you made to Creator
To always defend me, and now
Together in thanksgiving
Our song of honour we sing

the tree

She goes alone, to the ancient tree
The same where a child had bounced
On her father's knee
The same that gave Kòkomis shade
The tree which witnessed
A promise made
The tree recalled the woman say
That in its presence
She would confide and pray
When depression submerges her heart in pain
The tree brings again, the beauty
Of God's domain

the leaves

The rich earth of my ancestral homeland
Waits patiently
To receive the leaves
And the richness of their flavours

The autumn moon
Has again made her promise
Obedient leaves, contrast with colour
For a while at least
Clatter, chatter
While the kiss of the robin
Signals to all it is time
To cover the forest floor with nourishment
And again, the earth is fed

leaf-bearing trees

The leaf-bearing trees of late summer
Look weary
Outwardly they appear to be
In a state of growing weakness
But it is just an illusion
The trees remain as strong
As when the leaves were green and vibrant

I am as a leaf-bearing tree

I stand strong, my roots, my bloodline
Rising from the rocky earth
I catch the wind
And speak my words of thanksgiving
My knowledge of the Good Spirit
Stronger now
Than in my younger years

worthy

I will turn my face
Towards the sun and say
Grandfather
In your fire I find my strength

I will allow the winds
To gently stroke my thoughts
And I will say
Father
O how you make me wise

I will gaze upon
The full circle of the moon
And say
Grandmother
Through you I see
The love of God

I will lay down
On soft meadow grasses
And say
Mother
Heal me and teach me
To respect all the things
On this earth

And only after I have done
All of these things
Will I be worthy
To walk among the trees

COVER PHOTO ARTIST

CATHERINE DALLAIRE

Catherine Dallaire was born in 1979 in Kitchener, Ontario and currently resides in Waterloo, Ontario. She is Métis with roots in both the Kichesipirini band of Algonquin (Allumette Island) and the Weskarini band of Algonquin (Trois-Rivières). She is a multidisciplinary visual artist whose work possesses unique form and energy, balancing elements and teachings from traditional Woodland art/Métis and Anishinaabe art & culture with contemporary techniques and subjects. Many of her works challenge the viewer to examine deeply ingrained beliefs about the natural world that have been instilled in us by colonization, strive to call to attention the importance of our connection to our plant and animal relatives, and remember the original teachings that they carry. Catherine mainly works in acrylics, watercolour, porcupine quills, birchbark, caribou and moose hair, antler, beads and leather. She is an avid supporter of various initiatives by the Onaman Collective, No More Stolen Sisters, and Save the Evidence. One of her favourite things is corn soup and she will gladly accept a bowl of corn soup with bannock. More of her work can be seen at cdmetisart.com.